UCHICAGO**CCSR**

THE UNIVERSITY
OF CHICAGO
CONSORTIUM ON CHICAGO
SCHOOL RESEARCH

I0157465

RESEARCH BRIEF NOVEMBER 2012

Designing and Implementing the Next Generation of Teacher Evaluation Systems

Lessons Learned from Case Studies in Five Illinois Districts

Bradford R. White, Illinois Education Research Council and **Jennifer Cowhy, W. David Stevens, Susan E. Sporte**, University of Chicago Consortium on Chicago School Research

TABLE OF CONTENTS

Acknowledgements

The authors gratefully acknowledge participation from Elgin District U-46 , Evanston/Skokie CC District 65, Niles Township High School District 219, Olympia CUSD 16, and Sandoval CUSD 501. We appreciate those teachers, district administrators, and principals who were willing to make time to openly share their experience and wisdom with us. Without their cooperation and support, this project could not have happened. We also thank Jennifer Barnhart from the Illinois Education Research Council and Mengge Ji and Valerie Michelman from the University of Chicago Consortium on Chicago School Research (CCSR) for providing research assistance.

We would also like to thank members of our Advisory Committee for their suggestions based on our early findings. In addition, members of the CCSR Steering Committee, Peter Godard, Lila Leff, Karen G.J. Lewis, Stacy Norris, and Arie van der Ploeg, provided thoughtful and important feedback on an earlier draft. Stacy Ehrlich provided helpful insights throughout the process, and Elaine Allensworth, Emily Krone, Bronwyn McDaniel, and Eliza Moeller also provided in-depth critique that greatly improved the final report.

This work was funded by a generous grant from the Grand Victoria Foundation. We thank them for their support of this timely project.

This report was produced by UChicago CCSR's publications and communications staff: Emily Krone, Director for Outreach and Communication; Bronwyn McDaniel, Communications and Research Manager; and Jessica Puller, Communications Specialist.

Graphic Design: Jeff Hall Design
Photography: Jeff Hall, Cynthia Howe, and David Schalliol
Editing: Ann Lindner

11-12/pdf/jh.design@rcn.com

Executive Summary

In a very short period during the spring and summer of 2012, researchers at the University of Chicago Consortium on Chicago School Research (CCSR) and the Illinois Education Research Council (IERC) collected data from respondents in five districts across Illinois to examine how school districts in the state approach designing and implementing new teacher evaluation systems. Drawing on research in these districts, which are located in north, central, and southern Illinois, this report describes the challenges experienced across the districts. In addition, we present strategies the districts used to address these challenges as they occurred and their reflections on lessons learned:

CHALLENGE 1
Cultivating Buy-In and Understanding

- **Gather All Perspectives:** Stakeholders may be more likely to buy into evaluation systems—and the evaluation policy is more likely to improve—if they play an active role in developing its components, and if their feedback is incorporated throughout implementation.

- **Develop a Shared Vision of Quality Instruction:** Creating clear, common, and high standards for teacher performance can facilitate productive collaboration between teachers and administrators. It can also help focus principals and teachers on what matters most for improving student learning.

- **Train Teachers Early, Consistently, and Continuously:** Early and continuous training can help ensure that personnel throughout the district receive consistent information about the evaluation system. Training can also help facilitate teachers' understanding of the importance of the system and how it works.

- **Align Evaluation Reforms with Other District Initiatives:** Thoughtful and intentional alignment can reduce the perception that the new evaluation system will be burdensome or undercut other important district initiatives.

- **Start Soon and Implement Gradually:** Early and gradual exposure to new teacher evaluation systems can reduce anxiety and promote general understanding about its components.

CHALLENGE 2
Using Evaluations for Instructional Improvement

- **Build Evaluator Capacity:** Well-trained observers can more effectively and more accurately distinguish between levels of teacher performance, set clear expectations for teachers, and provide productive feedback on practice.

- **Link Observations to Professional Development:** Coupling evaluation with professional development can drive improvement goals and focus support for teachers at all levels of performance.

- **Conduct More Observations:** Observing teachers multiple times per year can help alleviate concerns about the accuracy of ratings, build teacher trust, and promote improvement.

CHALLENGE 3
Reducing the Burden on Principals

- **Streamline the System:** Reducing the logistical demands placed on evaluators can help them conduct more observations, be more efficient, and focus on improvement.

- **Use Multiple Observers:** Using multiple trained evaluators can reduce the time demands placed on principals and improve the reliability of ratings.

Incorporating Student Growth into Teacher Evaluation Systems

- Although the majority of case study districts have not yet integrated student growth measures into their evaluation systems, the plans, experiences, and concerns of all five districts help illustrate the most challenging aspects of this issue: ensuring fairness and rigor across all subjects, incorporating multiple assessments that are reliable and valid, and helping teachers and principals understand how to use assessment data for school improvement.

Implications

For all that has been accomplished by these case study districts, teacher evaluation, in all cases, remains a work in progress. Many in our interview sample described ongoing issues and some complicated problems. The report synthesizes these issues and raises some key questions for districts to consider around three common themes: teacher and principal support, communication, and buy-in; ensuring that ratings are accurate and consistent; and developing high-quality student assessments:

- How can districts clearly communicate expectations to teachers and ensure all teachers understand the new system?

- How might districts and principal preparation programs provide support for principals to build the new skills required for instructional leadership and performance management?

- How can these new evaluation systems be organized to provide differentiated supports for teachers at all levels of skill and all levels of experience, as well to promote the dissemination of best practices?

- How can districts create processes to ensure that raters are consistent so teachers can trust the fairness of the system?

- As districts throughout Illinois work to design and implement student growth models, how can the state provide sufficient support to help them develop high-quality assessments that are valid and reliable?

- How can districts find the time and opportunity to learn from one another and to make use of each other's expertise?

As we move forward as a state in developing performance measures, it will be important to continue to monitor the various designs described here, as well as others that continue to evolve. As similar reforms become more widespread nationally and we begin to learn more about the successes (and failures) from both inside and outside Illinois, we will have additional opportunities to build on these early lessons and answer these outstanding questions.

Introduction

The Performance Evaluation Reform Act (PERA), which was signed into law in January 2010, requires that every district in Illinois adopt new teacher evaluation systems that address both teacher performance and student growth.[1] The teacher performance measures required by PERA must include both formal and informal classroom observations, as well as associated professional development. For student growth, the law defines various qualifying assessment types and combinations of assessments that must be used. Teacher performance and student growth ratings must then be combined to create a single summative rating of teacher performance. PERA will be phased in over the next four years, starting with the lowest-performing schools, Race to the Top participants, and School Improvement Grant recipients, progressing to state-wide adoption by the beginning of the 2016–17 school year.

Given the imminent implementation of PERA, researchers from the University of Chicago Consortium on Chicago School Research (CCSR) and the Illinois Educational Research Council (IERC) set out to investigate Illinois districts that have already incorporated features of this reform. The goal was to draw on the insights and experiences of these trailblazing districts to provide important lessons for other Illinois districts as they work to implement PERA requirements.

This project began with a scan of 13 districts recommended by state organizations with broad knowledge of Illinois' teacher evaluation landscape—the Performance Evaluation Advisory Council (PEAC), Illinois State Board of Education (ISBE), Large Urban District Association (LUDA), Advance Illinois, and Consortium on Educational Change (CEC). We then selected five districts, based on diversity in geography and district size, student demographics, and stage of implementation, for in-depth case studies of how Illinois districts approach designing and implementing new teacher evaluation systems. The districts selected for these case studies were: School District

U-46 (Elgin), Evanston/Skokie CC School District 65 (Evanston), Niles Township High School District 219 (Niles), Olympia CUSD 16 (Olympia), and Sandoval CUSD 501 (Sandoval).

These five case study districts represent a variety of approaches to teacher evaluation and are in various stages of planning and implementation. All of the case study districts used Charlotte Danielson's Framework for Teaching as their teacher performance measure, and all had worked to various extents with the Consortium for Educational Change in designing or training for their teacher observation components.[2] Only one district (Evanston) included student growth measures in their teacher evaluation system at the time of our interviews. **Table A.1 in Appendix A** of this report provides more details on the characteristics of these districts and key components of their teacher evaluation policies.

Each case study district utilized an evaluation committee to design a new teacher evaluation system. We interviewed four to six committee members in each district, speaking with central office administration (33 percent of our sample), principals or other evaluators (26 percent), and teacher representatives (41 percent).[3] Most participants were still involved as leaders as their district implemented the teacher evaluation reforms. Interview questions focused on the policy design process, implementation, and perceptions of the new system. Responses from interview participants reflect their individual perspective as a member of a district design team. They are not necessarily indicative of widely held views in the case study districts. Details of the study's methodology, including district scan and case study interview questions, appear in **Appendix B** of this report.

Below we summarize the experiences of the case study districts, highlighting the lessons they learned for supporting the development of teacher evaluation systems. Specifically, we describe the three major challenges that these districts faced—and other districts are likely to face—as they design and implement new evaluation systems for teachers: cultivating buy-in and understanding, using evaluations for instructional improvement, and reducing the implementation burdens on principals. We then describe concrete strategies the case study districts used to address these challenges. In addition, we describe the districts' ongoing questions as they begin to incorporate student growth into their systems. The *"district spotlights"* scattered throughout these sections highlight promising and innovative approaches from each of the case study districts. We conclude with a section on unanswered questions that remain on the road ahead. This report is not intended to be an evaluation of existing plans or progress in these districts. Rather it provides illustrations of common obstacles and guidance for how to navigate them.

Cultivating Buy-In and Understanding

Across all five case study districts, respondents reported that buy-in to the new evaluation systems was less than ideal, especially in the first year of implementation. In particular, teachers and administrators from several districts viewed teacher buy-in as a weak link and noted that teachers needed more trust in their system for these policies to reach their full potential. In addition, respondents in many districts felt training for the new evaluation system focused primarily on principals or evaluators, and that more attention should have been paid to helping teachers understand these new systems. Teachers in several case study districts said that they were initially briefed on the changes to the evaluation system, but there was little follow-up or ongoing training beyond these introductions. Several teachers reported that some of their peers still felt uncomfortable with their new evaluation system and did not fully understand the processes and standards embedded in their district's plan. As one teacher said,

> "[Teachers] have an idea of what they think is good teaching, but do they know specifically what's on the form and what are the different dimensions and what are the different...descriptors? The vast majority of people haven't put that kind of thought [into it]. It's something we're working on. I mean, we see that as being a problem that we want to address. How do we educate people when we have so many other things going on, you know?"

In a few districts, a history of distrust between teachers and administration was an initial obstacle. Some respondents also noted that the looming requirements of PERA combined with Senate Bill 7, which links teacher evaluation ratings to tenure and employment decisions, have added a new dimension to teachers' anxiety. In addition, some teachers in the sample were cautious about the reactions that might occur as districts transitioned from an old system where everyone was rated highly to a new system where this might not be the case, particularly for underperforming teachers who may have been told for years that their work was satisfactory.

Finally, many teachers and administrators noted that the success of these systems was also highly dependent upon principal understanding and buy-in, as well as the degree of trust and openness between principals and teachers in their buildings. These factors, too, proved to be a challenge for some schools in these districts. For example, one observer noted that up to a third of the principals in his district had yet to fully embrace the system. Further, he added, teachers whose administrators did not accept or understand the system had a hard time buying in themselves because they found it difficult to trust a system in which their administrator did not believe. As a result, implementation varied widely within some districts.

Below, we provide five strategies that these districts used to help principals and teachers embrace and understand these new systems, and we illustrate these lessons with examples from two of the case study districts.

Gather All Perspectives

Superintendents and union leaders in these districts both observed that the proper composition of the policy design team was crucial. In most districts, they worked to ensure that the evaluation design committee had members that represented diverse perspectives and different roles, schools, content areas, and grade levels. Many committee members felt they were selected to participate in the committees because they wore multiple hats in the district and could represent several constituencies. Some respondents also noted that teachers were much more likely to buy into new evaluation plans if they originated from other teachers, rather than by administrative fiat, and teachers from most of

5

the case study districts reported that they believed they had a strong voice in policy design.

Many respondents also emphasized that the process of gathering input from multiple perspectives should not end with the policy design phase. Several districts incorporated formal monitoring structures and appeals processes into their evaluation systems and noted that these structures helped build trust in the system by ensuring that they could adapt to changing needs. Some districts also found it helpful for the evaluation committee to remain intact through early implementation to ensure continuity and regularly re-evaluate the policy. These standing evaluation committees (along with program staff in districts with the resources to create such positions) were charged with monitoring implementation, gathering feedback, and communicating concerns to the appropriate parties to ensure the systems were working as designed.

In fact, it was common practice in these districts to make additional policy changes as more input was gathered during implementation. Although respondents noted that these alterations were welcomed because they typically helped to improve the system, they recommended that districts avoid making major policy changes during the school year in order to prevent unnecessary confusion and concerns about fairness.

Train Teachers Early, Consistently, and Continuously

Interviewees in these five districts noted that communicating the new evaluation system to district educators beyond the design committee was *"huge,"* and that translating the policy from the original committee to the rest of the school community has often been a challenge. Respondents recommended that districts begin communicating during the policy design phase, when teachers will likely hear that a new evaluation system is forthcoming and rumors about the contents of this policy may begin to form. To address these issues, subjects in the case study districts recommended email updates, informational Q & A sessions, and speaking openly about the work of the joint committee in order to inform teachers and administrators about what to expect when the new policy is implemented.

Several interviewees recommended beginning to train teachers on the new policy at the end of the year before it is to be implemented, if at all possible. For example, Evanston introduced their plan by providing emails and presentations in the spring and summer prior to implementation, with principals offering additional training at the beginning of the first year of implementation. According to one teacher, *"they wanted every teacher to get the exact same message about it—and they did an outstanding job on this. And it was presented at staff meetings throughout the district."* Similarly, Sandoval designed their teacher performance measure during the year prior to implementation and offered initial training in the spring with additional workshops in the weeks leading up to the first year of implementing the new observation protocols, and the district will follow this same timeline for design and rollout of their student growth measure over the course of the next year.

In a few districts, some or all of the training for teachers in the new evaluation system was conducted on a voluntary basis. While some interviewees said such teacher choice was empowering, others said many teachers were simply not aware of the significance and relevance of this training and, as a result, teachers in these districts report that their peers' understanding of the evaluation system lagged. According to one teacher, the initial training in his district was *"just a staff meeting depending on how well your principal understood it…And he just went over it in an hour, and that was the only training our teachers had in it."*

Several respondents suggested that, at the bare minimum, teachers need several hours of training on their new observation standards and rubrics, as well as time with their evaluators to discuss what distinguishes the various performance levels. A few principals commented that this was particularly true for veteran teachers, since the systems were such a big change from the way they had been doing things for years. One strategy to mitigate such concerns was evident in Sandoval, where all teachers and principals who will be using the new system were required to participate in all four of CEC's teacher evaluation training modules prior to the first year of implementation.

Facilitating Teacher Evaluation Reform in Sandoval CUSD 501

Sandoval is the newest teacher evaluation system included in this report and was in the planning stage of their efforts during the study period. In 2010, the district received a School Improvement Grant (SIG), which helped to support their teacher evaluation design work. The SIG provided Sandoval with the resources to hire a facilitator from the Consortium for Educational Change (CEC) who has assisted the district's evaluation committee through the design phase. Committee members noted that the use of a facilitator has been a vital part of the success of their design process by helping to plan the work of the committee and providing access to key examples of similar work from other districts. In addition, the facilitator helped the design committee identify common goals about teacher evaluation. The three core beliefs that have guided Sandoval's policy design work, and which feature prominently in the teacher evaluation resources created to communicate the policy to the rest of the district, are as follows:

1 *"An effective evaluation system will help us provide our students with effective teachers.* Research shows that effective teachers make the biggest impact on the quality of our students' educational experiences. We will do everything we can to give all our teachers the support they need to do their best work because when they succeed our students succeed. With effective evaluation systems, we can identify and retain excellent teachers, provide useful feedback and support, or intervene when teachers consistently perform poorly.

2 **Teachers are professionals, and our evaluation system should reflect that.** We have created an evaluation system that gives teacher regular feedback on their performance, opportunities for professional growth, and recognition when they do exceptional work. We're committed to evaluations that are fair, accurate, and consistent. The new system will ensure that evaluations are based on multiple factors that paint a complete picture of each teacher's success in helping students learn.

3 **A new evaluation system will make a positive difference in teachers' everyday lives.** Novice and veteran teachers alike can look forward to detailed feedback that is tailored to the individual needs of their classrooms and students. Teachers and evaluators will meet regularly to discuss successes and areas for improvement, set professional goals, and create an individualized professional growth plan to meet those goals."

As in the other districts in this study, the leadership of a program champion helped to bring teacher evaluation to the fore and keep it there. The superintendent wanted the district to be a state leader in teacher evaluation and to be involved in the creation and development of their new evaluation system. Her view was, *"If we don't do this work, somebody else is going to, and we'd rather be involved in the creation than just given the tool."* While the SIG served as a catalyst, the evaluation committee in Sandoval credited the superintendent's proactive approach for positioning the district to receive the grant.

Through the joint leadership of the superintendent and facilitator, the Sandoval evaluation committee has made rapid progress in designing a teacher evaluation system. Committee members cited a sense of ownership and accountability in the process, as well as a feeling that all voices were well represented. In return, representatives from Sandoval have visited numerous other local districts to share their plans and experiences in order to help their peers implement PERA reforms successfully

Respondents in some of districts observed that additional questions are likely to arise even after the initial rollout stage, as new teachers enter the district or as policy modifications occur. These participants recommended holding regular teacher evaluation training sessions at the beginning of each year as part of new teacher orientation or back-to-school institute, where teachers and administrators can exchange questions, answers, and advice. They also recommended providing new evaluators with access to previous teacher evaluations in order to understand district-specific language and expectations. Finally, they suggested ongoing teacher evaluation system updates through district or union newsletters and other regular communications.

Align Evaluation Reforms with Other District Initiatives

Several interviewees said that teachers and principals in their districts were often concerned about the additional workload brought on by the new evaluation systems, especially at a time when they already felt overwhelmed by other mandates and initiatives. As a result, even when teacher evaluation was of highest priority to district administrators, it did not always translate to being the highest priority in buildings and classrooms. In one district, a teacher commented that much of their reform energy had been *"sapped up"* by other ongoing initiatives. In another, a principal noted that many teachers were mostly consumed with the immediate concerns of the additional workload and the potential consequences of the new evaluation system, instead of viewing it as a potential lever for change and instructional improvement.

To relieve this concern, some administrators commented that other reform initiatives could be aligned to, or pursued in the context of, the teacher evaluation framework. One suggested that the evaluation system can serve as *"the glue that holds all those other pieces together"* if it is used as a vehicle to integrate other district initiatives. Another principal said that, because teacher evaluation aligns so well with other district initiatives, nothing has to take a back seat to or share center stage, and that teacher evaluation could be used to enhance these other initiatives by serving as a means of measuring their progress.

The case study districts provided several examples of this sort of intentional alignment between teacher evaluation components and ongoing initiatives in the case study districts. For example, Olympia sought to hire principals with previous experience in similar evaluation systems and developed a teacher hiring protocol to measure the skills embedded in the Danielson Framework in order to determine person-organization fit and increase buy-in to the district's teacher evaluation system. Other locales used the policy design phase to customize their evaluation system to support district goals that were already in place. For example, one district customized elements of the teaching standards to reflect strategies from other ongoing professional development activities:

> "When we...constructed [wording of] the new evaluation tool, what we did was, we tried to take the different things that are going on in the district...the things that we value, whether it's racial equity, whether it's using technology in classrooms, differentiated instruction, whatever. There were different things that we as a district value and we really tried to build it into the evaluation tool, and by doing that, really sort of cementing it for us as a district."

As an example, this interviewee went on to describe as specific teaching standard that her district modified:

> "The dimension is about teaching strategies...it's very broad...so we fleshed it out so that it literally states...'literacy, differentiated instruction, assessments of learning practices' so these were all terms that people within the district are aware of, had had training in, are hopefully using in their own classrooms, and so then a really sort of generic dimension like teaching strategies becomes distinctly '[our district].'" [Administrator]

Start Soon and Implement Gradually

Representatives from multiple districts noted that it was difficult for teachers to fully understand the new evaluation system until they had experienced it, and that it was impossible to predict what changes to policy and process might be required until the system had been rolled out. For example, one district administrator noted:

> "Well I think that this isn't something that teachers are going to understand until they do it. So you can try to prepare them and try to prepare them, but...all of the training in the world isn't going to help them until you are actually doing it. So I think it was a good decision to go forward with it, and I think...in the first year, we were conscious of that...and supportive of people as they went through the process."

For these reasons, teachers and administrators in some districts recommended that the new evaluation policy be piloted or phased in over multiple years, at lower stakes, in order to ease anxiety and to make the adjustments that might be necessary to fine-tune the plan before full implementation. Several respondents noted that teacher buy-in increased considerably once teachers saw that those in the pilot program were satisfied with the new plan. For example, subjects in one district noted that there was initial anxiety about the new plan because it was unknown, while their old systems were viewed as quite harmless: *"For most people, the old evaluation system was benign. It was there, once every two years, if your administrator does his or her job, they come in and do the evaluation, zip, zip you're done."* They found that this initial anxiety tended to wane once the new observation system was implemented and the first wave of teachers experienced success. Interviewees also noted that phasing in the system could provide a better idea of the system's capacity for such major change.

Because it takes time to pilot and incorporate feedback, many administrators in the case study districts emphasized the importance of beginning the teacher evaluation design process as soon as possible to allow sufficient time to build capacity before the deadline for full PERA implementation. However, it should also be noted that some respondents mentioned disadvantages to longer phase-in periods. For example, rolling out a plan over several years could mean an extended and complicated period of trying to manage two parallel evaluation systems as teachers transition from the old plan to the new.

Develop a Shared Vision of Quality Instruction

Interviewees stressed the importance of developing a shared vision of instruction, and many of them noted that the evaluation policy design process itself was one of the greatest successes of these new systems, precisely because it provided a venue for teachers and administrators to come together to discuss instruction and the supports that were needed to improve teaching and learning across the district. The central office administrators, principals, and teachers interviewed in these districts sought change, and leadership from both teachers and administrators provided the impetus for the design and implementation of new systems in these districts. Every district in our case study wanted to design a formative teacher performance assessment that could create a common language around quality instruction.

Simply the act of adopting clear and commonly agreed upon teacher performance standards and rubrics (in the case of all of these districts, Charlotte Danielson's Framework for Teaching) was also viewed as helpful for catalyzing collaboration between teachers and evaluators by many of the participants in our study. In particular, numerous teachers and administrators felt the observation process provided a venue for constructive conversations about *"what really matters"* and a common language to discuss these issues. Further, they noted that these productive discussions around instruction had previously gotten sidetracked by other issues in the absence of a shared teacher performance framework.

9

Alignment and Phase in to Build Buy-In and Understanding in Elgin U-46

Elgin's path toward creating a new teacher evaluation system began with the realization the district's well-regarded, Danielson-based mentoring program was not aligned with or supported by the evaluation system their teachers would experience once they earned tenure. In response, the leadership of the teacher mentoring team became the driving force behind reforming the district's teacher evaluation system, and the teachers union seized the opportunity to become pioneers in formative evaluation reform. By moving to a teacher appraisal system that was also based on Danielson's Framework, they were able to leverage the knowledge and skills developed through the mentoring program to bolster their capacity to implement teacher evaluation reform—the performance standards were already accepted by a large proportion of the district's teachers, and a cadre of capable evaluators had already been established. Thus, by building on this existing strength, Elgin was able to reduce both the costs of additional training and any potential resistance to the new evaluation system.

Elgin representatives also reported success with the strategy of using teacher-administrator teams to visit each school in the district and introduce the policy to teachers and administrators simultaneously. Both teachers and administrators whom we interviewed reported that this joint training helped to ensure that all parties received consistent information and worked toward greater collaboration on the process:

"We sent out teams, so it was two people doing the training. It was a teacher and an administrator together, and that was one of the biggest pieces...and, with that process, an administrator was trained with their teachers, so everyone heard the same message coming from both sides at the same time, and that was so valuable." (Teacher)

"What we did really well in those initial trainings was the administrators were in the same rooms with the teachers, and they were delivered collaboratively with the teacher and administrator. Minimally that perception piece was important, but there was a shared belief system about what that meant." (Administrator)

In addition, the director of the new evaluation system (who had previously led the district's mentoring efforts) was able to secure two full-time staff for the program, along with additional support re-allocated from the district instructional technology department. Elgin phased in their system through voluntary participation, adding approximately one-third of the district's teachers each year between 2008 and 2011. By fall 2012, they had completely phased out their old evaluation system and were fully implementing the new system district-wide.

Using Evaluations for Instructional Improvement

Most teachers in the case study districts thought that their new evaluation system helped hold other colleagues more accountable by creating a common language with clear standards around quality instruction. Teachers in the study sample generally felt that the performance standards and rubrics of the Framework were, in the words of one participant, *"crystal precise"* and were appropriate for all teachers regardless of grade level or subject area. Both teachers and administrators supported this movement away from the old system of checklists and *"dog and pony shows"* that they believe was broken, and toward attempts to get a more accurate picture of classroom instruction. As one administrator noted: *"[Teachers have] seen their district going in a positive direction, and now…the teachers are holding each other accountable for higher standards, and that increases the climate and the culture and the morale. And those who don't want to be with us anymore are leaving."* School administrators in particular liked that their new teacher performance assessments explicitly set clear and high expectations for teachers, with no surprises and without *"playing gotcha."*

Several respondents noted, however, that while the new teacher evaluation systems are excellent at pinpointing teachers' weaknesses, they were less successful at helping transform those weaknesses into strengths. In general, respondents said that teachers in their districts craved honest, informed feedback on their craft and did not shy away from constructive criticism. At the same time, several principals and evaluators said the most difficult piece of these systems was having *"tough conversations"* with teachers about how to address their weaknesses, figuring out the next steps once these weaknesses had been identified (including professional development workshops), and coaching teachers to help them progress from one performance level to the next.

In addition to uncertainty about whether evaluators would be able to effectively use observation ratings to focus on instructional improvement, numerous responses from administrators, teachers, and principals pointed to concerns with the validity and accuracy of evaluation ratings as a major weakness of these systems. Representatives from almost every district in the study identified potential subjectivity or lack of inter-rater reliability as a persistent flaw in their systems. In some districts, respondents worried about perceived rating inflation or accusations of favoritism; in other districts, they were concerned about lack of fidelity to the system or inadequate training and preparation.

Though every case study district intended to use the Framework in a formative way, teachers worried that the looming requirements of PERA combined with Senate Bill 7, which links teacher evaluation ratings to tenure and employment decisions, would shift people's focus to accountability rather than improvement. As one teacher noted, there is worry that this shift in focus could lead stakeholders to overlook some of the more promising features of these new evaluation systems:

11

"There's so much talk about evaluation and finding those teachers who shouldn't be in the classroom, and…I think it's best used in the reverse. What this does, it identifies the teachers who are most competent, who have the best practice. Before, they had no idea…. I mean, you have someone in your building you knew was a really good teacher, but what was it about them? What was it about their practice that…possibly others could benefit from? So, now we have that information, and hopefully the district leverages it…. To me, that's more important…you're going to find some teachers who need to be doing something else, and there's a way to humanely do that, and I think the new system allows for that. But the biggest benefit is learning from those who are highly skilled at teaching."

In addition, some respondents cited the tension between meeting the needs of both high- and low-performing teachers as a challenge, especially when deciding how to integrate professional development into the evaluation system. Teachers in the sample noted that their peers at all levels of performance, not just those who were struggling, would appreciate honest feedback about how to improve their practice. In the experience of some teacher respondents, positive summative ratings were often ignored, while those identifying clear areas for improvement were usually acted upon appropriately. Some districts considered whether professional development should only be required for struggling teachers or if all teachers should be devising professional growth plans. Some representatives felt that, if the goal of the new system was to improve teacher practice, every teacher should attend development workshops; while others felt this approach could be too prescriptive for high-performing teachers; and some districts in the sample are still struggling with how to integrate this component.

Below, we provide some examples of successful strategies used in the case study districts to help increase system capacity to ensure the teacher evaluations are used to improve teacher performance. We describe three broad strategies these districts used to help promote teacher growth and illustrate these lessons with an example from a case study district.

Build Evaluator Capacity

Extensive principal training was often a focus in these case study districts, and principals were generally satisfied with their training and support in the new observation systems. Some districts utilized trainers from the Danielson Group or the CEC, while others used independent consultants or hand-picked trainers from within the district. This initial training typically consisted of multiple modules lasting between 12 and 35 hours over several days, and focused on helping evaluators understand the observation process and teaching standards and tools; distinguish between various teacher performance levels; collect appropriate evidence; and provide formative feedback.

Several veteran evaluators stated that their most valuable training experiences came through in-teractions with other evaluators, particularly in jointly observing and rating teachers, either in person or on video. In general, administrators in the sample felt such experiences helped them to calibrate their ratings and feel more confident in their decision making. Evaluators in Niles and Sandoval used this approach, while administrators in Elgin used similar role-playing and mock observation exercises. According to an evaluator in one of these districts, *"the best way to do it is just have them look at things, have them watch videos, and come together and talk about...what's good teaching and what's not good teaching."* One evaluator even recommended undertaking these calibration exercises multiple times each year to ensure that all evaluators remain on the same page. One evaluator also suggested that "anchoring" exercises, where evaluators view prototypical examples of teacher performance at various levels, were underutilized tools that could also be a useful tool in this arena.

In districts that have not done these formal calibration exercises, respondents report that mentorship and discussions amongst evaluators have helped to maintain some degree of consistency and common understanding of good teaching. Evaluators generally valued what time they were given to discuss the system with other administrators, and often wished they had more time and opportunity to interact with their fellow evaluators. As one evaluator said, *"I think just the only [other] thing that I would do [is] go through the evaluation with another administrator the first time or the first couple of times through, just to make sure that I was kind of on the right track."* It should also be noted here that PERA evaluators are required to be trained and certified through the Growth through Learning process provided by the Illinois State Board of Education in conjunction with CEC. Multiple subjects in this study suggested that this state-sponsored training—particularly the Teachscape video review module—could help with this inter-rater reliability.

Link Evaluations to Professional Development

In general, respondents felt their teacher evaluation systems were strongly aligned with district goals and initiatives for teacher growth and helped reinforce the view of evaluation and professional development as a *"cycle"* to help teachers identify areas for improvement and plot a plan for growth. As one district administrator put it, *"I tell…the people designing PD, everything has to come from the judgments of the pattern of strengths and weaknesses identified by people who are responsible for their teaching, for leading that effort every day."* For example, according to interviews in Evanston, district administrators are making good use of these new data on teacher performance and student growth, and they are planning their professional development based on the weaknesses identified in their teacher performance measure.

Other case study districts are also using data management systems to move beyond tracking compliance and toward using data to help improve their instruction. For example, Olympia uses evaluation ratings along with staff surveys to determine where to target professional development offerings. Representatives from other districts noted that the coaching model provided by the Danielson Framework could be easily adapted to specific professional development activities occurring in local districts. Elgin examines which teaching standards are being evaluated during formal and informal observations to determine whether educators are focusing on current district objectives and also to drive evaluator training:

> "I began using that information to drive the administrator training that went on for three years. I was training them off their practice. 'Here's what you're telling me you're doing, here's what you're really doing, here's where I see some gaps and holes…here's what you should be doing, and here's what you're telling me through some different avenues that you need training on.' So from that, I was able to make really relevant training for them, PD which they love…because, again, it's structured…specifically tailored to their needs. It's not just somebody coming in saying, 'You need this.' You know? It's their practice." (District Administrator)

Conduct More Observations to Obtain Better Ratings and Build Trust

Many subjects noted that some issues with the validity and reliability of ratings could have been resolved if evaluators had spent more time observing classrooms. Teachers from several districts noted that evaluators need to be in their classrooms much more often in order to offer productive feedback and for their ratings to be accurate and formative. One union representative also pointed out that, while some teachers would just as soon be evaluated as infrequently as possible, his association actually encourages frequent observations in order to catch problems early and provide teachers opportunities to improve. Another teacher observed that frequent, unannounced observations—if evaluators were trained in this technique—could be more valuable and accurate and more likely to result in growth than formal evaluation visits. Some principals also recommended that their fellow evaluators spend more than the bare minimum amount of time in teachers' classrooms, noting that most evaluation policies do not *"lock principals out of the classroom"* by forbidding further informal observations. One principal also welcomed the idea of adding a peer evaluation component to the evaluation repertoire. Some district administrators also echoed these concerns, noting that evaluators need to spend more time in classrooms in order for educators to trust the system. If teachers feel that the feedback they receive is inaccurate, they note, they will not trust the evaluators' ratings. And, because they do not trust the ratings, these teachers are less likely to feel the need to improve in areas their evaluators perceived as weak.

13

Building a Formative Evaluation Culture in Olympia CUSD 16

Respondents from Olympia report that the culture they have developed around their evaluation system includes comfort, collegiality, trust, conscientiousness, and a willingness to share. The superintendent cultivates this culture and is a strong mentor for the district's principals. He trained all of the district evaluators and read every teacher evaluation. He occasionally joins principals on their informal observations of teachers and regularly visits their offices to review the evaluation policy, answer questions, offer advice, and help with interpretation. When teacher-training needs are identified through the evaluation system, he makes sure that the district pays for professional development.

The principals with whom we spoke were appreciative of this formative atmosphere and took their responsibilities seriously:

> "All the mentoring that goes on in the district administratively...everyone's pretty connected to each other, and [the superintendent will] give us literature that's helpful for us to read. We have all the Danielson books and all the frame-works for teaching. And the updated version, I actually just finished reading last night because there's another administrator that wanted to read it before we had gone through the required 32 hours of video modular training."

One principal is quite renowned through the district for his lengthy, detailed observation reports, which provide feedback on every evaluation component along with suggestions for moving to the next level. One principal offered to join the district's newest principal on evaluation rounds to walk through the evaluation process and tools together and help him start off on the right track. In addition, some district principals have one-on-one meetings with all of their new teachers to explain the evaluation process to them and develop personalized evaluation schedules. New principals have access to the teacher evaluations scored by the previous administrator in order to track teachers' growth and allow them to continue working on personal goals.

In turn, according to respondents, many teachers in Olympia tend to have great trust in their evaluators and do not fear their evaluators or dread the evaluation process. In fact, teachers are typically the ones saying the evaluators need to push for more, observe classrooms more frequently, and have more unannounced visits to hold them more accountable.

However, as some respondents noted, Olympia's atmosphere of comfort and collegiality could be interpreted as lack of prioritization or urgency by some in the district. That is, the absence of stress, and having an evaluation system that is viewed as a *"non-issue"* or *"not a topic of conversation"* other than days when teachers are getting observed, or where *"most who get good summative ratings just throw it in a drawer"* is viewed as not necessarily a good thing. Similarly, teachers' requests for observations and more unannounced visits were also interpreted by some respondents as indicators that the system needs more "push for growth."

Reducing the Burden on Principals

As many teachers in the interview sample pointed out, the ultimate impact of these systems is largely dependent upon principals and their implementation of these systems. As one teacher put it:

> "[It is] how the administrator proceeds through that is equally as important as the evaluation tool, because if this evaluation tool still becomes just that checklist, which it easily can...then, you know, it's no different really than anything we've done in the past. But if the administrators truly embrace it as an opportunity to provide that growth—and that's a lot of responsibility on their part because that's going to take more time on their part."

This concern was shared by numerous school administrators in the study, who noted the additional responsibilities these new evaluation systems placed on principals. These administrators pointed out that principals are asked to serve as classroom observers— sometimes the only observers (**see Appendix A**)—in these systems, and many principals were concerned about the degree to which they would be required to perform more frequent and more thorough classroom observations than they had in the past. In addition, several subjects felt that these new evaluation systems held principals more accountable for performance management and for prioritizing instructional leadership. Numerous principals also noted that competing priorities and *"daily realities"* of the principalship made it difficult to prioritize teacher evaluation reforms to the extent required to achieve their full potential.

The logistics of implementing these systems also presented challenges in some case study districts. While some observers received training on the more practical aspects of the evaluation system, such as how to schedule and organize evaluations over the course of

the year, and found it quite useful, others had trouble adequately pacing their observation responsibilities. As a result, some evaluators occasionally had to rush to fit multiple classroom visits into a small timeframe at the end of the school year in order to meet policy requirements. And since non-tenured teachers were often viewed as the primary focus of these evaluation systems, observations for tenured teachers were occasionally put off or given short shrift, which proved problematic if these teachers' struggles were not identified until late in the year.

Recognizing the increased load that this new observation system placed on principals, several districts in this study tried to find ways make implementation easier for school administrators. Below, we describe two strategies that were used to reduce the burden on principals, and we illustrate one successful approach with a brief case study.

Streamline the System Wherever Possible

The case study districts developed several innovative strategies to reduce unnecessary implementation burdens and create more time to focus on instructional improvement. For example, in Olympia they recognized that their new evaluation system was quite *"paper-heavy"* and that some forms were cumbersome, but they also realized that tracking and utilizing all of the data from observations could be quite useful. So administrators invested in technology to ease the burden of both data collection and data utilization. They provided evaluators with iPads, software, and apps that allowed them to be more mobile while scoring lessons, to send immediate feedback to teachers via email, and to spend more time in classrooms and less time scripting on paper and converting those scripts onto forms on their desktop computers. In addition, some principals in Olympia worked together to develop personalized calendars for each teacher, which outlined the evaluation schedule for the entire year and made it easier for both teachers and principals to devote adequate time to fulfill required procedures and adhere to deadlines.

Olympia and Sandoval have also created implementation toolkits and guidebooks for teachers. These documents were distributed to all staff members, and numerous respondents felt they served as a useful reference to help simplify and summarize the more complex teacher evaluation policy document and make the process more user-friendly. Tools such as these are also important because, as noted in several districts, following proper processes and procedures are areas where principals often stumble. This is particularly problematic because these areas may be grieved under the teaching contract, while evaluation content typically is not permitted to be grieved.

Elgin has gone completely paperless with their evaluation system and uses online tools and forms that provide automatic, real-time feedback and submission of data to the appropriate audience (teachers or the central office), and they are quite satisfied with the results. According to one central office administrator:

> "It's one of the pieces that made the whole program successful. It isn't so much about the values and beliefs of the program—which I think are essential in this document—but these are enhancing pieces that allow user ease. And when you make something easy to use, it becomes less threatening and you don't have that undertow, and then the document can take over and you can begin doing the good work."

Use Multiple Observers

Though few of the case study districts were able to utilize multiple evaluators or to use individuals other than the principals as classroom observers, those that were able to do so found this quite helpful for reducing the burden on any single individual. Some districts occasionally use assistant principals to observe some staff members to help lighten the load on principals (**see Appendix A**). Niles is one district that has managed to both increase the number of classroom observations and alleviate the burden on principals by hiring additional evaluators. They were able to fund release time for two "consulting teacher" positions to serve as full-time evaluators and coaches for their Peer Assistance and Review (PAR) program, which both provided support to teachers and alleviated burden on principals.

Using Peer Assistance and Review to Build Capacity in Niles Township High School District 219

Around 2008, the president of the Niles Township Federation of Teachers learned about a Peer Assessment and Review (PAR) program in Toledo, OH, where experienced "consulting teachers" were used to evaluate and support new teachers. After some time exploring the PAR program and visiting Toledo, teacher leadership in Niles eventually persuaded district administrators to adopt the program, and the district completed its first full year of implementation in 2011–12. Under this system, every first- and second-year teacher in the district is observed eight to 12 times per year. At the end of the year, their cases are presented before a PAR panel composed of five teachers and four administrators, who ultimately recommend renewing or dismissing each teacher. Under the previous system, respondents suggested that Niles principals simply had too many teachers to supervise effectively. By carving out funds for two consulting teachers to observe and support new teachers, the PAR program in Niles has helped observers feel much less overwhelmed by their caseloads.

The educators interviewed in Niles were also excited about PAR because they felt it helped professionalize teaching and brought instruction to the forefront of employment decisions: *"We see ourselves as academics, we see ourselves as educated people with high standards for our profession, and we would like to have some control over our profession."* The administration credits PAR with changing the district's climate around evaluation to allow for serious conversations around good teaching. Despite concerns that teachers would exercise extreme leniency in evaluating their peers, respondents in Niles noted that this was far from the case. In fact, they argue that teachers actually have higher expectations than administrators because they—not administrators—are the ones who have to deal with the consequences of poor instruction by having to re-teach content that students should have previously mastered. In fact, they note, teachers want to work with high-quality peers whose work will support and reinforce their own instruction. As one Niles educator put it:

"We can't control the hiring process but we can make sure they become great teachers in their first and second year, and if they're not great teachers, to be very frank, then we make sure they don't stick around...We had some situations in the past where they hired not the best, strongest candidate, and that person worked in our district for three or four years... [and] they made it through their first [year], all strong evaluations; for their second year, all strong evaluations; for the third year, all strong evaluations; and then the fourth year, all of a sudden, they're held accountable, and then they're let go...because no one said to them, 'This is what you're doing wrong and how you can get better.' That's totally wrong, and so I have a lot of confidence in PAR that the consulting teachers don't care [who you are], they're going to come in, they're not trying to fire you, but they're trying to help you become a better teacher."

Importantly, the PAR program incorporates ways for teachers to improve their instruction by allowing new and struggling teachers to learn from experienced and respected teachers. New teachers in Niles are also assigned a mentor from their department for additional instructional support. As a result, subjects in Niles argued that the PAR system, with its numerous observations and associated supports, actually made it easier to dismiss struggling teachers:

"They like PAR because PAR helps [administrators] make the tough call...[So] then they can say, like, 'It wasn't [me]. It wasn't my director or my principal. The, you know, the PAR thing did it.' And, so they like that, too. [It] frees them up a little bit to release some of these people who they don't think are the strongest teachers."

PERA has provided the impetus for the administration and union in Niles to come together again around improving the district's evaluation system. As a result, the PAR program is expanding this year to address the needs of veteran teachers in need of improvement, and the program has grown to include four full-time consulting teachers.

17

ACT: Reading

Incorporating Student Growth into Teacher Evaluations

The Big Unanswered Question

Integrating student growth into next generation teacher evaluation systems is one of the most challenging hurdles that remain for most of the case study districts. Only one of the five districts, Evanston, had fully integrated this component into their teacher evaluation system at the time of this study. The districts that have yet to incorporate a student growth component are aware that they must do so soon, but, as one teacher observed, these design committees have been reluctant to *"be the ones inventing the whole wheel."* Nonetheless, the experiences in Evanston (as illustrated in the **District Spotlight:** *Using Student Growth to Align Teacher Evaluation*) and other case study districts that have already started down this path can provide some valuable guidance.

Niles has considerable experience using student growth measures, but solely for purposes of program evaluation and improvement. Because of this, district representatives feel they are well-positioned to incorporate student growth into their teacher evaluation system, since teachers and administrators are now familiar and comfortable with these measures. Niles has been using the EPAS series of assessments from ACT, Inc., along with district-wide end-of-course (EOC) assessments, and they have already worked to establish a historical track record of growth trends for students in their district. One district administrator reported that this process has given them information on teachers and students that national or state norms cannot:

> "[It] gives us our own local data and help[s] us make decisions on how students are achieving, under which teachers...We're dealing with our teachers in our schools in our situations and what would it be and how would it be, for example, if the child were in a different school, with a different teacher, in a different district."

Administrators in Niles stated that they did not want to wait for a state student growth model of unknown quality, so they decided to pilot their student growth component for teacher evaluation in the English, math, and physical education departments this school year; student growth will be fully integrated into their system ahead of the state deadline.

Sandoval will be working with their facilitator throughout the 2012–13 school year to design the student growth component of their teacher evaluation system, and the district hopes to roll out the new student growth plan this spring, along with professional development days devoted to communicating the new tools and setting goals for growth. As several members of the evaluation committee noted, it will also be important for the district to establish a new Common Core-aligned scope and sequence in all areas of the curriculum, before they are able to make solid plans for student growth measures.

Teachers throughout the case study districts shared many concerns about the use of student growth for evaluation, especially when attached to high-stakes decisions, such as tenure or compensation. Some worried about ensuring fairness and rigor across all subjects, speculating that improving student growth in some grades, subject areas, or student populations may be more difficult to accomplish than in others. A related concern was that some disciplines simply do not lend themselves well to growth measures, either because they currently lack a valid and reliable standardized assessment infrastructure (non-tested subjects) or because of the non-sequential nature of their subject matter. Other teachers voiced doubts about whether some assessments were valid measures of teacher performance. For example, some teachers in our sample felt that existing tests could not measure skills that they endeavor to impart, such as critical thinking and citizenship, or that atypical teaching situations (such as non-classroom positions) might lead to insufficient sample sizes, misattribution, or other technical concerns. A few teachers in the sample also noted concerns that an overemphasis on student test scores could lead teachers to narrow the curriculums or cheat to produce desired results.

The majority of teachers and principals, including some who voiced concerns about these issues, were accepting of the fact that linking student growth to teacher evaluation was imminent. Thus, they were more concerned about the strategies and supports that would be put in place accompanying these systems in order to overcome these perceived weaknesses and make the growth component as fair and formative as possible. Teachers throughout the case study districts advocated using multiple measures to evaluate student growth, including student portfolios, teacher-created curriculum-specific assessments, and locally normed assessments, along with standardized, nationally normed tests.

PERA's requirements for multiple student assessment types are also in line with these recommendations. In addition, many teachers and principals with whom we spoke stressed that understanding how to use standardized assessment data and how to set appropriate goals for every student's growth were also imperative.

For their part, several district administrators were aware that there were concerns about the use of student growth in teacher evaluation. Some administrators attributed at least part of this resistance to what they perceive as teachers' limited understanding of student assessment, growth models, and PERA's student growth requirements. For example, in one district there were rumors that 70 percent of a teacher's evaluation score would be based on student growth. Once it was effectively communicated that PERA would only require student growth to account for 30 percent (at most) of their evaluation ratings, teachers' fears subsided.

Using Student Growth to Align Teacher Evaluation with District Goals in Evanston/Skokie CC School District 65

Evanston is the only district in this study that currently uses student growth as part of its teacher evaluation system. The Evanston plan incorporates NWEA MAP assessments, as well as departmentally developed assessments for subjects without MAP tests. District administrators in Evanston believe that this component has brought students to the forefront of the evaluation conversation and helped teachers understand the relationship between their practices and student growth. They view the growth component as vital in aligning their teacher evaluation system with board goals for student achievement. District administrators also note that a well-designed student growth component can address some of the perceived weaknesses of the No Child Left Behind accountability system by focusing on the whole class, rather just subgroups of students or those at the borderline of proficiency. Further, Evanston has used the student growth component as a professional development tool to help boost teachers' knowledge of assessments, which was viewed as a district-wide need. Administrators say they hope that teachers' experience with the student growth component can help them learn what to look for in a quality assessment so they can choose or design better performance measures for their students. The growth component in Evanston is also used to reinforce the district's notion of accountability—that teacher performance is related to student growth, and, as such, that teachers are responsible for ensuring that each student makes one year's growth in one year's time.

District administrators in Evanston regularly examine the distribution of teacher performance ratings to see how they compare with the distribution of student growth in the district, and they work with principals to ensure that these two measures square with each other. In fact, district administrators view the two components as quite complementary to each other. They note that the observation component is important because it can help explain student growth outcomes and it can help identify potential issues before the growth data become available. As the results of Evanston's teacher performance ratings become more closely aligned with their student growth measures, district leaders stated that they hope to use observation data to pinpoint particular teacher actions that are linked to student gains.

Evanston teachers, on the other hand, noted several difficulties with implementing the student growth component. Some concerns centered on large fluctuations in student growth scores, which led them to question the reliability of the NWEA MAP. Other concerns were with regard to the training and support that were available to help teachers interpret the student growth results. District leaders in Evanston are still trying to determine the best way to combine teacher performance and student growth into an appropriate summative score and questions remain about which assessments provide valid and reliable evidence of student growth, how to develop comparable assessments across various disciplines and content areas, and what constitutes adequate yearly growth. These issues have been further exacerbated by the district's efforts to link evaluation results to teacher salaries (in some instances) and to raise the bar for student growth to align with college and career readiness standards. As a result of these ongoing challenges and unanswered questions, subjects report that many Evanston teachers feel that the student growth component is difficult to understand, and some believe it is not fair to include this component in their teacher evaluations until the questions are resolved.

Summary and Implications

The Illinois Performance Reform Act (PERA), with its requirement that teachers be evaluated by a combination of teacher performance observations and student growth, represents a marked change in teacher evaluation processes for most districts in the state. The experiences of the five case study districts indicate that such change is possible, but that it is an ongoing process with few one-size-fits-all solutions. While representatives of all five districts indicated that the evaluation system they now have is better than their old one, they also described areas that required continuing oversight.

Representatives from these districts generally believe that teachers and administrators have worked well together to craft an evaluation system that fits the needs of their district. Respondents across all five districts indicated that the formative parts of the new observation process have, in general, succeeded in providing a venue for encouraging teachers and administration to collaborate, have serious discussions around instruction, and develop a common definition of and framework for achieving quality instruction. They have been able to use teacher evaluation as a way to align other district policies, creating more coherence instead of only adding work.

Below, we summarize the lessons these districts presented about how to address some common obstacles. The summary is presented in the order that districts are likely to encounter these challenges—first during policy design, then during training and rollout, and finally during implementation and monitoring.

STAGE 1
Policy Planning and Design

- **Gather All Perspectives:** Stakeholders may be more likely to buy into evaluation systems—and the evaluation policy is more likely to improve—if they play an active role in developing the components and if their feedback is incorporated throughout implementation.

- **Develop a Shared Vision of Quality Instruction:** Creating clear, common, and high standards for teacher performance can facilitate productive collaboration between teachers and administrators. It can also help focus principals and teachers on what matters for improving student learning.

- Align Evaluation reforms with other district goals: Thoughtful and intentional alignment can reduce the perception that the new evaluation system will be burdensome or will undercut other important district initiatives.

- **Start Soon and Implement Gradually:** Early and gradual exposure to new teacher evaluation systems can reduce anxiety and promote general understanding about its components.

STAGE 2
Communications, Training, and Support

- **Train Teachers Early, Consistently, and Continuously:** Early and continuous training can help ensure that personnel throughout the district receive consistent information about the evaluation system. Training can also help facilitate teachers' understanding of the importance of the system and how it works.

- **Build Evaluator Capacity:** Well-trained observers can more effectively and more accurately distinguish between levels of teacher performance, set clear expectations for teachers, and provide productive feedback on practice.

Implementation

- **Link Observations to Professional Development:** Coupling evaluation with professional development can drive improvement goals and focus support for teachers at all levels of performance.

- **Streamline the System:** Reducing the logistical demands placed on evaluators can help them conduct more observations, be more efficient, and focus on improving instruction.

- **Conduct More Observations:** Observing teachers multiple times per year can help alleviate concerns about rater reliability, build teacher trust, and facilitate improvement.

- **Use Multiple Observers:** Using multiple trained evaluators can reduce the time demands placed on principals and improve the accuracy of ratings.

Questions for Consideration

Yet for all of this progress, teacher evaluation in all cases remains a work in progress; many in our interview sample described ongoing issues and some complicated problems. In light of these comments, we raise the following questions for consideration:

1. Respondents from several districts named communication with teachers and their understanding of the new system as a weak link. Even though there was general agreement that teachers need a thorough understanding of the standards and rubrics so that they know what they should be striving for to improve their instruction, some district representatives described how leaving this important piece of the effort solely up to principals led to inconsistent results.

   How can districts augment this potential communications gap? Can administrators and teachers unions find ways to mutually share vital information with teachers?

2. There was almost universal agreement that principals play a crucial role in helping these systems reach their full potential, and that to effectively carry out this complex task principals may have to acquire new skills and priorities. Specifically, principals will need to be able to do more than accurately rate teaching performance—which is a monumental task in itself—they will also need to be able to provide concrete guidance to teachers about how to improve their practice. In addition, some respondents also indicated that teachers in buildings whose principal had not bought in to the system would be unable to participate fully in the new evaluation system.

   How might districts and principal preparation programs provide support for principals to build the new skills required for instructional leadership and performance management? How might districts identify and change the outlooks and behavior of resistant principals?

3. Respondents in several districts also expressed some concern about a potential lack of consistency in ratings across buildings and across time. Some of the case study districts had practices in place for evaluators to discuss ratings with each other and some have suggested undertaking calibration exercises several times a year.

   How can districts create processes to ensure that raters are consistent so that teachers can trust the fairness of the system? How can the system be organized to allow for the maximum number of observations to increase the precision of ratings, teachers' trust in their accuracy, and the utility of the feedback provided?

4. Several districts observed that the evaluation system needs of struggling teachers were quite different than those of the high performers, and that these systems tended to focus primarily on identifying weak teachers or weak teaching practices, rather than learning from best practices and improving the practice of teachers at all levels.

   How can these new evaluation systems be organized to provide differentiated supports for teachers at all levels of skill and all levels of experience, as well to promote the dissemination of best practices?

5. Only one of these districts has fully incorporated student growth metrics into its teacher evaluation system, and even in this district the growth component that is used does not formally incorporate the multiple measures and specific assessment types that will be required under PERA. Another district will be expanding its use of student growth from program evaluation to include it as part of teacher evaluation in 2012, while a third is currently preparing to include student growth as part of teacher evaluation in 2013. Therefore, this report is unable to document specific strategies that have been useful in successfully implementing PERA-compliant student growth plans. Nonetheless, it does provide some insights from those who have begun to think about the challenges and strategies that will need to be addressed in a comprehensive way statewide.

   As districts throughout Illinois work to design and implement these student growth models, how can the state provide sufficient support to help them develop high-quality assessments that are valid and reliable? How can they ensure that these new assessments are able to meet the diverse needs of teachers and students throughout the state?

6. These five districts (and others from across the state) have had to rely largely on themselves, external consultants, and out-of-state prototypes for advice and guidance. The advent of PERA will mean that all districts in Illinois will now need to be working toward a common goal of designing and implementing these next generation teacher evaluation systems, which brings great opportunities for state-support, economies of scale, and sharing of ideas.

   How can districts find the time and opportunity to learn from one another and to make use of each other's expertise? How will the challenges facing districts that undertake these initiatives voluntarily differ from the obstacles that face those that adopt the programs less willingly?

Moving Forward

Given the flexibility PERA allows for districts to design their own combinations of measures for teacher performance and student growth, it is likely that Illinois will see a wide variety of new evaluation systems, some that look very similar to those described in this study, and others that present new innovations. As we move forward as a state, it will be important to continue to monitor these various designs. Will one model of teacher evaluation emerge as preferable or superior to others? Will some strategies work better for certain contexts, such as urban or rural districts? Will these models be equally valid and reliable? And perhaps most importantly, which models will be most successful at helping to improve student achievement? As similar reforms become more widespread nationally—with more aggressive timelines spurred through federal Race to the Top incentives and similar initiatives in other states—and we begin to learn more about the successes (and failures) from both inside and outside Illinois, we will have additional opportunities to build on these early lessons and answer these outstanding questions. We are hopeful that the experiences and perspectives provided in this report can help all Illinois districts maximize the full potential of PERA and teacher evaluation reform.

Appendix A

Matrix of Teacher Evaluation Program Characteristics

TABLE A.1

Geography and Demographics					
	Elgin U-46	**Evanston/ Skokie CCSD 65**	**Niles Township High School District 219**	**Olympia CUSD 16**	**Sandoval CUSD 501**
Geography	North	North	North	Central	South
Locale	Urban	Suburban	Suburban	Rural	Rural
Number of Schools	54	15	2	5	3
Student Enrollment	40,689	6,642	4,730	1,894	542
Grade Span	PreK-12	K-8	9-12	PreK-12	PreK-12
Percent of Low-Income	52%	40%	31%	32%	69%
Percent of White Students	33%	44%	46%	95%	96%
Percent of Black Students	7%	26%	7%	1%	1%
Percent of Hispanic Students	49%	19%	12%	2%	0%
Percent of Asian Students	8%	5%	31%	1%	0%
Percent of Student Mobility	12%	6%	4%	9%	21%

Evaluation System					
	Elgin U-46	**Evanston/ Skokie CCSD 65**	**Niles Township High School District 219**	**Olympia CUSD 16**	**Sandoval CUSD 501**
First Year of Planning	1998	2008	2008	2004	2010
First Year of Implementation	2008	2008	2011	2005	2012
Size and Composition of Evaluation Committee	16-20 (diverse)	20 (10 administrators and 10 teachers)	9 (5 administrators and 4 teachers)	10 (3 administrators, 1 board member, 6 teachers)	7 (3 administrators and 4 teachers)
Use of Facilitator	No	Yes (CEC)	No	No	Yes (CEC)
Teacher Performance	Yes	Yes	Yes	Yes	Yes
Evaluation Tool	Modified Danielson	Modified Danielson	Danielson	Modified Danielson	Modified Danielson
External Training for Observation Instrument	Yes (CEC)	Yes (CEC)	Yes (CEC)	Yes (CEC)	Yes (CEC)
Student Growth	No	Yes	Piloting in 2012-13	No	Designing
Other Measures	No	No	No	No	No
Growth Measures	—	NWEA/MAP, District EOC Assessments	Beginning 2012-13: ACT EPAS, District EOC Assessments	—	TBD
Number of Levels	4	4	4	4	4
Number of Formal Evaluations for New Teachers	3 per Year	2	8 to 12	1	3 observations and 9 meetings
Number of Informal Observations for New Teachers	1 per Year	1	Not Specified	1	Not Specified
Number of Formal Observations for Tenured Teachers	1-2 Every Other Year	1	2	1	1 observation and 1 meeting every other year
Number of Informal Observations for Tenured Teachers	Not Specified	Not Specified	Not Specified	1	Not Specified
Who Observes?	Principals and Other Administrators	Principal and/or Outside Evaluator	Peers and Administrators	Principals/APs	Principal
HR Link	Remediation Plans	Salary, PD	PD, renewal	Hiring, renewal	PD, tenure

Note: District demographics are 2011 data from the Illinois Interactive Report Card (http://iirc.niu.edu/).

Appendix B
Methodological Notes and Protocols

This study used a qualitative case study approach to gather and analyze data. Starting in Spring 2012, we identified case study sites using a judgment sample (or reputational case selection) by asking representatives from state organizations with broad knowledge of the Illinois teacher evaluation landscape—the Large Unit District Association (LUDA), Performance Evaluation Advisory Council (PEAC), Illinois State Board of Education (ISBE), Advance Illinois, and Consortium for Educational Change (CEC)—to nominate districts they viewed as leaders in implementing teacher evaluation reform. Thirteen districts were named in this process, and we conducted initial half-hour screening interviews via telephone with program leaders in the districts who were willing to participate in the study. These policy scans helped to determine basic policy features and suitability for study. The full policy scan interview protocol is included at the end of this section of the report. We then used the information gathered in these policy scans and endeavored to select case study districts that would be representative of the geographic and demographic diversity of the state, as well as illustrative of the range of program components and implementation stages that districts are likely to encounter throughout the teacher evaluation policy design process. Through this process we identified five sites for case study: School District U-46 (Elgin), Evanston/Skokie CC School District 65 (Evanston), Niles Township High School District 219 (Niles), Olympia CUSD 16 (Olympia), and Sandoval CUSD 501 (Sandoval).

In each of the case study districts, we interviewed four to six key individuals identified by the program leader, including teachers, union representatives, principals and other evaluators, and district administrators (**see Table B.1**). Interviews were conducted during the summer of 2012 and lasted approximately one hour each. Questions focused on the policy design process, implementation, and perceptions of the system; and the full case study interview protocol is available at the end

of this report. All interviews were transcribed, and data were coded using ATLAS.ti analytical software. Earlier versions of this report were reviewed by the districts to ensure accuracy and clarity.

TABLE B.1

Case Study Districts and Participants

District Name	Interview Participants		
	District Administrator	Evaluator	Teacher
Elgin District U-46	3	1	2
Evanston/ Skokie CCSD 65	3	0	3
Niles Township High School District 219	1	2	1
Olympia CUSD 16	1	2	2
Sandoval CUSD 501	1	2	3

District Policy Scan Protocol

STRUCTURE

1. What measures are included in your teacher evaluation system? (observations, student growth, other measures?)

2. (If multiple measures) How are these combined and how much weight is given to each?

DESIGN/DEVELOPMENT

3. How long did this process take from planning to implementation?

4. Who was involved in the teacher evaluation design process and how well did these various stakeholder groups work together? (i.e., collective bargaining issues, work groups, and decision making, etc.)

TEACHER PERFORMANCE

5. What teacher evaluation tool/framework was chosen? How many performance levels are on the observation rubric?

6. How many observations and what types of observations (e.g., how often, formal/informal, announced/unannounced, duration—walk-through, full lesson, full day) are required?

7. Who conducts the teacher observations? (principals, teams, peers, etc.) Do they receive any training?

STUDENT GROWTH

8. Does the district mandate/recommend specific growth measures?

9. How many and what types of assessments are used in determining student growth?

10. Are all teachers included in this component of the evaluation system, or just those in tested subjects and grades? If the former, what measures are used for those in non-tested subjects and grades?

ADDITIONAL MEASURES

11. What are the additional measures?

USE, IMPACT, AND REPORTING

12. How are evaluation results used: Inform PD? HR decisions (such as promotion, dismissal, renewal, tenure, or compensation)? Career ladder or to identify teachers for roles such as mentor teachers, master teachers, etc.?

CLOSING

13. What is the biggest strength of your teacher evaluation system?

14. What is the biggest area for improvement?

15. Is there anything else you would like to tell me about why it would be important for other districts trying to implement new evaluation systems to study your district's experiences?

District Case Study Protocol

BACKGROUND

1. Can you tell what your job title is and what you do?

2. How long have you been in this position?

3. How long have you been working in the district?

EVALUATION SYSTEM

4. I want to spend a little bit of time making sure I understand all of the components of your evaluation system. [Spend five minutes reviewing/confirming/adding to what we learned from the initial scan. Interviewer will add the specific questions to this section given what he knows and what he needs to learn.]

5. Would you say the emphasis of the system is on formative or summative (improvement vs. accountability) purposes? Does the district require/allow evaluation results to be used in human resource decisions such as promotion, dismissal, renewal, tenure, or compensation? If yes, what conditions require/allow evaluation results to trigger promotion, retention, dismissal?

IMPETUS AND GOALS

6. What was the district's impetus for developing the new evaluation system?

7. What did district administrators hope to accomplish? Teachers union? Principals? Teachers?

8. How is the evaluation system aligned to the district's strategic plans or other reform initiatives?

9. Considering all of the district's strategic plans or other ongoing initiatives, how high of a priority does the district place on teacher evaluation?

PARTICIPANTS

10. Describe the various stakeholders involved in the teacher evaluation design process.

11. Who is/was included in the process (on committees, etc.)? Who is/was not included?

12. Whose feedback is/was solicited? (pilot participants, teachers, etc.)

13. Do you have a sense of how the interests or needs of different participants overlapped or conflicted? Can you tell me about them?

14. Describe your role in the teacher evaluation design process.

15. Was this part of your job or an added responsibility?

16. How did you become involved in the process?

PROCESS

17. Describe the process of designing the teacher evaluation system. (Probe to get details on the design process including: What happened first? Design activities, coordination process, major decisions/tradeoffs, decision making process, communication)

18. How well did the various stakeholder groups work together? (Probe on collective bargaining issues, structure of work groups and decision making, conflicts)

19. What are the successes so far in the design process?

20. What have been the challenges so far in the design process?

21. Timeline (how long did this all take)?

22. What were/are the costs of the new evaluation system? (start-up and ongoing administration)

23. How was it funded? (district, state, school reallocation, etc.)

24. Were there any challenges around funding the system?

IMPLEMENTATION

25. What is/was the timeline for rolling out the system?

26. How was the broader school community educated or informed about the new evaluation system?

27. Has the communication process worked to produce a good understanding of the system?

28. Do you think teachers and evaluators buy in to the system?

29. What are teachers in your schools saying about the evaluation system?

30. Would you say that all stakeholders have been given sufficient time, training, and other resources and support to successfully implement this initiative? If not, what additional supports and resources do you think they need?

31. Overall, what would you say are the strengths of your teacher evaluation system?

32. What are areas for improvement?

33. Are there any plans for ongoing monitoring or evaluation of the system?

34. Are there any plans to change the system or add or subtract any particular aspects?

CLOSING

35. As we are working to document this effort of building a state teacher evaluation system, what documents do you think are critical for us to collect to understand this work? From whom could we get these documents? (CEC, TNTP, ISBE)

36. Is there anything else you would like to tell me about the evaluation system? Any important lessons to pass on to other districts trying to implement new evaluation systems?

Endnotes

1. PERA also requires new principal evaluation systems, which are not addressed in this report.

2. Danielson's Framework is also being used as the default state teacher performance assessment; CEC, with whom many of these districts consulted, is a local expert in the design and implementation of this model.

3. See Table B.1 in Appendix B of this paper for further details on participants from each district.

ABOUT THE AUTHORS

BRADFORD R. WHITE is a Senior Researcher with the Illinois Education Research Council located at Southern Illinois University Edwardsville, where his work focuses on supporting effective teachers and principals throughout Illinois. Prior to coming to the IERC, he conducted research on innovative teacher evaluation and compensation systems with the Consortium for Policy Research. He earned his MA in Educational Policy Studies from the University of Wisconsin-Madison in 2001.

JENNIFER COWHY is a Research Assistant at CCSR. Her research interests include: early childhood, community schools, roles of educational support personnel in student learning and youth development, and school reform. Her current research involves teacher-quality and human capital. She received her BA with distinction from the University of Michigan and is currently pursuing an MPP and an MA from the University of Chicago's Irving B. Harris School of Public Policy and School of Social Service Administration.

W. DAVID STEVENS is Director for Research Engagement at CCSR. His current research interests include the transition into high school and teacher preparation. He also develops trainings and workshops for helping practitioners, policymakers, and school districts understand CCSR research findings and use them in their daily practice. Stevens received his PhD in sociology from Northwestern University.

SUSAN E. SPORTE is Director for Research Operations at CCSR. Her current research focuses on teacher preparation and measuring effective teaching. She serves as the main point of contact with Chicago Public Schools regarding data sharing and research priorities; she also oversees CCSR's data archive. Prior to joining CCSR, she worked as a community college math instructor, field evaluator for a not-for-profit agency, and college administrator. She received a BS in mathematics from Michigan State University, an MA in mathematics from the University of Illinois at Springfield, and an EdM and EdD in administration, planning, and social policy from the Harvard Graduate School of Education.

This report reflects the interpretation of the authors. Although CCSR's Steering Committee provided technical advice, no formal endorsement by these individuals, organizations, or the full Consortium should be assumed.